Aran the Home Visiting Pharmacist

by Sufiya Ahmed
Illustrated by Noopur Thakur

Contents

OXFORD
UNIVERSITY PRESS

Meet Aran!

I am a pharmacist.

Aran

Pharmacists hand out medicines to patients, and tell them how to take the medicines safely.

One day when Mamba was swimming
down the river she saw a fish.
SNIP!
went Mamba
at the fish.

Then Mamba saw a frog.
SNAP!
went Mamba
at the frog.

Then Mamba saw a bird.
SNIP!
SNAP!
SNIP!
went Mamba
at the bird.

'Don't do that, Mamba!' said
Mum and Dad Crocodile.
'That is the crocodile bird. He is
our friend. You must not do that
to the crocodile bird.'

'But I could eat up that bird in one
SNAP!' said Mamba.

'No, you must not do that, Mamba,'
said Mum Crocodile.

'Look at your dad. He will show you
what to do.'

Mamba looked at Dad Crocodile.

She saw him open his big mouth.

The crocodile bird flew in.

'Dad is eating the crocodile bird,'
said Mamba.

'No, he isn't,' said Mum. 'Look again.'

Then Mamba saw what the bird was
doing. It was eating all the bits
of food on Dad Crocodile's teeth.
Dad Crocodile didn't eat the bird
because he wanted to have clean teeth.
'Thank you, crocodile bird,' he said.
'Now, Mamba, look at your mum.'

Mamba looked at Mum Crocodile.
She saw her open her big mouth.
The crocodile bird flew in and
cleaned her teeth.
'Thank you, crocodile bird,' said Mum.

'Now you open your mouth,' said
Mum Crocodile to Mamba.
So Mamba opened her big mouth
but when the bird flew in, she shut
her mouth with a SNAP!

'Mamba! Open your mouth now,'
said Mum Crocodile.
Mamba opened her mouth and
the crocodile bird flew out as fast
as it could.
'I don't want clean teeth,' said Mamba,
'and I don't want the crocodile bird
as my friend.'

Then one day Mamba saw a giraffe
by the river.

'How are you, Mamba?' asked the giraffe.

'Oooooh!' said Mamba. 'My teeth hurt.'

'Then clean them in the river,' said
the giraffe.

Mamba tried, but her
teeth went on hurting.

Mamba went on down the river.

Next she saw a hippo in the water.

'How are you, Mamba?' asked the hippo.

'Oooooh!' said Mamba. 'My teeth hurt.'

'Then clean them with a stick,' said
the hippo.

Mamba tried, but her
teeth went on hurting.

Mamba went on down the river.

Then she saw a cheetah on the bank.

'How are you, Mamba?' asked the cheetah.

'Oooooh!' said Mamba. 'My teeth hurt.'

'Then clean them on a log,' said
the cheetah.

Mamba tried, but her
teeth went on hurting.

Mamba went on down the river.
She tried to forget about her teeth
but she could not. They hurt too much.
Then she saw the crocodile bird up
in a tree.
'How are you, Mamba?' asked the bird.
'Oooooh!' said Mamba. 'My teeth hurt.'

The crocodile bird flew down from
the tree.

'I'll clean your teeth,' said the bird,
'but please don't eat me.'

'No, I won't eat you,' said Mamba.

So she opened her mouth and the
crocodile bird flew in.

The crocodile bird ran all over Mamba's teeth and gave them a good clean. Mamba's teeth stopped hurting.

'Thank you,' said Mamba. 'Now I see why you are called the crocodile bird.'

And from that day on, Mamba and the crocodile bird were very good friends.

In Africa there was a beautiful river.
By the river were tall trees
and lots of green grass.
In the river lived a little crocodile
called Mamba.

Pharmacist or doctor?

Sometimes, you can get help from a pharmacist instead of going to the doctor. For example, if you have a sore eye a pharmacist can give you medicine to make you feel better.

However, if you are ill, you normally need to see a doctor first. The doctor will decide what medicine you need to get better. Then they will give you a special piece of paper called a prescription.

You take the prescription to a pharmacist like Aran. The prescription tells the pharmacist the name of the medicine and how much you need.

The pharmacist prints out instructions about how to take your medicine.

Warning!
Always follow the instructions. Too much medicine can make you more ill. If you take too little medicine, you might not get better.

Becoming a pharmacist

Aran spent four years studying at university. He learned about the human body and chemicals. He then trained at a pharmacy for a year. Finally, he had to pass some exams.

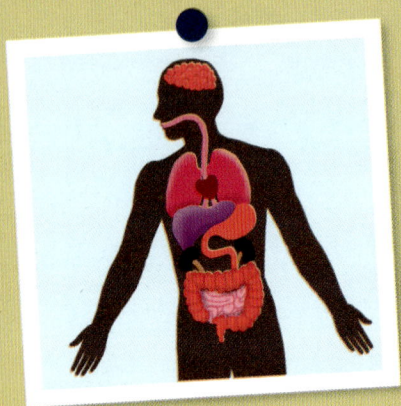

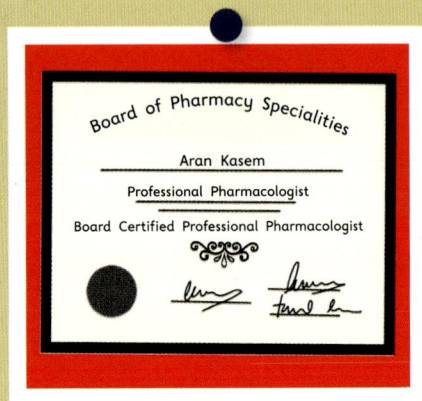

Board of Pharmacy Specialities

Aran Kasem

Professional Pharmacologist

Board Certified Professional Pharmacologist

At the pharmacy

Some people like to visit Aran at the pharmacy and pick up their medicine.

Salman has been to the doctor with his parents. He has a rash on his legs and needs to pick up some cream.

Home delivery

Some people need Aran to deliver their medicines to them. So, Aran makes time during his busy week to leave the pharmacy to visit these patients.

Aisha

First stop is eight-year-old Aisha. She loves to play football. She has diabetes.

Diabetes

Diabetes is when a person's body needs extra help to turn food into energy. Injections of **insulin** can help with this.

Aran is bringing her some insulin pens.

Last year, Aran taught Aisha's mum how to inject Aisha with the pen.

Annie

Aran's next stop is Annie, who has migraines.

> **Migraines**
> Migraines are painful headaches. The pain can last from a few hours to a few days.

Annie's cat is missing. She wants to put up reward posters outside, but the bright sunlight makes her headache worse.

Please can you do me a **favour**? Can you put up a poster outside?

Harry

Next, Aran visits Harry. Harry has a weak heart so he takes medicine to keep it beating properly.

A pain in one arm might be a sign of a heart attack.

> **Heart attack**
> A heart attack happens when the blood going to the heart gets blocked. Someone having a heart attack needs medical help straight away.

I've written down the medicine he's taking.

Clara

Aran visits Clara next. She has arthritis.

> **Arthritis**
> Arthritis is where bones and joints swell and cause pain.

Clara's hands, knees and hips hurt. She gardens to keep her joints moving.

Aran has some new medicine for Clara.
He explains that she will need to take
one pill every morning.

Peter

The next patient is Peter, who has asthma.

Asthma
Asthma is a problem with the lungs.
It can make breathing difficult.

Aran brings Peter a new inhaler. This helps open his airways so air can flow to his lungs.

Aran enjoys visiting Peter because Peter plays the guitar for him.

Samuel

Aran stops at the bakery before his last visit. At Samuel's house he hands over a white box and Samuel's medicine.

Three years ago, Samuel had a stroke.

Stroke

A stroke happens when a blood clot stops blood from getting to the brain.

He takes tablets every day, so this does not happen again.

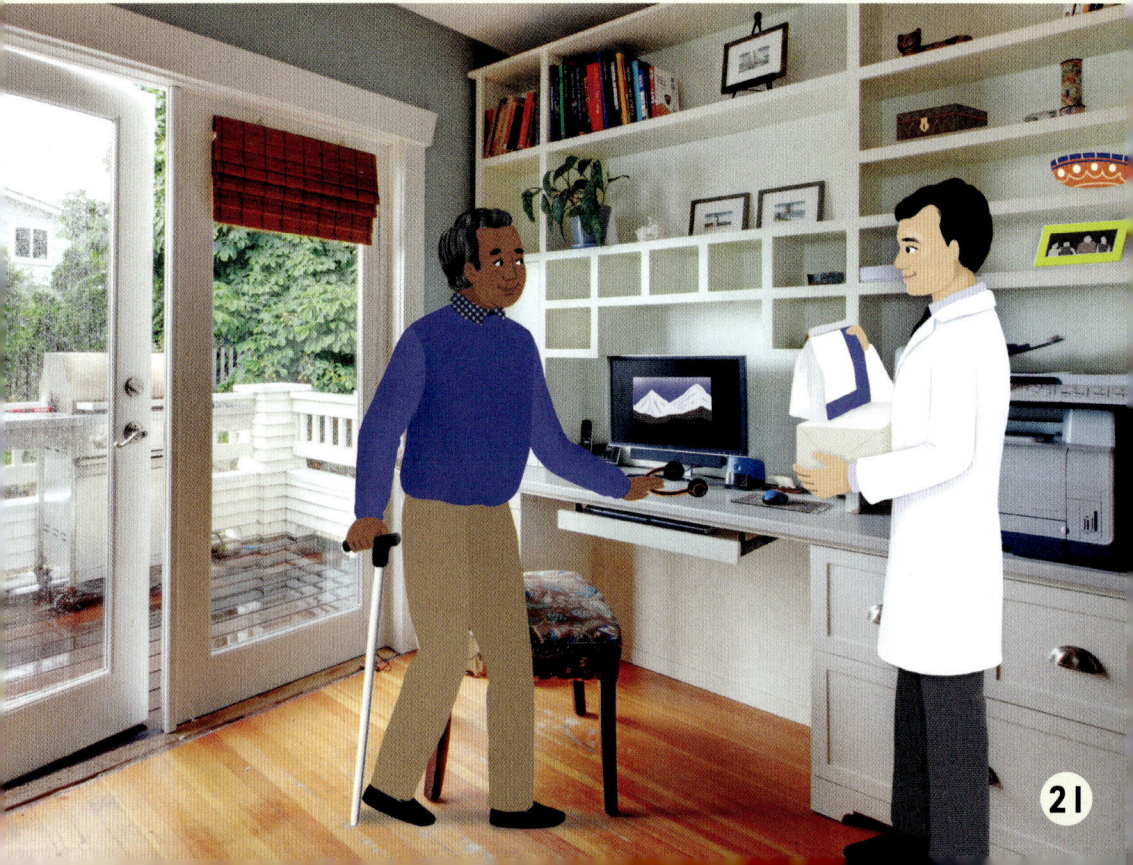

Samuel opens the white box. Inside, there is a birthday cake.

Shall we have a slice of cake now?

Happy birthday!

Health hero

Back at the pharmacy, Aran checks on Harry.

Harry was having a heart attack. Thanks to you, we got to the hospital in time. He's going to be fine.

Aran's patients **rely** on him for help and medicine. He keeps them healthy.

Glossary

favour: something kind that you do for someone

insulin: a chemical that controls how much sugar there is in the blood

rely: to trust someone to help you

Index

After reading

- Using the Glossary, make sure your child understands the meaning of all the words. Explain what the Index is for, and encourage them to use it.
- Talk with your child about the book. Here are some questions you could ask:
  - *Do you think Aran is a kind and caring pharmacist? Why?*
  - *Why do you need a prescription for some medicines?*
  - *Look at page 18. What is asthma? Why is an inhaler important if you have asthma?*
- Talk about some of the skills that you might need to be a pharmacist (e.g. sensitivity, empathy, good at communicating and listening).
- Encourage your child to read the book again. This will build their reading confidence and fluency.

Other things to do

Encourage your child to choose a medical condition. With support, role play together as a patient and pharmacist, asking your child to think about how a pharmacist would act and what they would say. Swap roles.

About the author

I am a children's author and live in London. I really enjoyed writing this book. My mother is house-bound which means she finds it hard to go out by herself. She has a wonderful home-visit pharmacist who delivers her medicine on time. It makes me feel better knowing that my mother is looked after well.

OXFORD
UNIVERSITY PRESS

Great Clarendon Street, Oxford, OX2 6DP, United Kingdom

Oxford University Press is a department of the University of Oxford. It furthers the University's objective of excellence in research, scholarship, and education by publishing worldwide. Oxford is a registered trade mark of Oxford University Press in the UK and in certain other countries

British Library Cataloguing in Publication Data

Data available

978-1-382-02952-0

10 9 8 7 6 5 4 3 2 1

Paper used in the production of this book is a natural, recyclable product made from wood grown in sustainable forests. The manufacturing process conforms to the environmental regulations of the country of origin.

Printed in China by Golden Cup Printing Co Ltd

Acknowledgements

The character featured in this book is a fictional character used to help portray the role of a real-life hero.
Illustrations by Noopur Thakur
Inside cover notes by Alison Slattery

Author photo courtesy of Sufiya Ahmed and Asif Patel Photography

The publisher and authors would like to thank the following for permission to use photographs and other copyright material:

Front Cover: Tom Werner / Getty Images; Cultura Creative RF / Alamy Stock Photo. Back Cover: Cultura Creative RF / Alamy Stock Photo. Photos: p2: Cultura Creative RF / Alamy Stock Photo; p3: Tom Werner / Getty Images; p4: New Africa / Shutterstock; p5: Tom Werner / Getty Images; p6: Tom Werner / Getty Images; p8: Tom Werner / Getty Images; p9: Tom Werner / Getty Images; p10: Antoha713 / Shutterstock; p11: Antoha713 / Shutterstock; p12: Edmund Sumner-VIEW / Alamy Stock Photo; p13: Edmund Sumner-VIEW / Alamy Stock Photo; p14: Photographee.eu / Shutterstock; p15: Ewelina W / Shutterstock; p16: Nick_Nick / Shutterstock; p17: Nick_Nick / Shutterstock; p18: Edvard Nalbantjan / Shutterstock; p19: Edvard Nalbantjan / Shutterstock; p20: Artazum / Shutterstock; p21: Artazum / Shutterstock; p22: Artazum / Shutterstock; and p23: Tom Werner / Getty Images.

Every effort has been made to contact copyright holders of material reproduced in this book. Any omissions will be rectified in subsequent printings if notice is given to the publisher.

Oxford OWL

Discover eBooks, inspirational resources, advice and professional development
www.oxfordowl.co.uk

Book Band 7
Turquoise

Oxford Reading
Level 7

Fully decodable
Letters and Sounds
Phonic focus: rare GPC
/ai/ (ea), /air/ (ar), /i/ (
/g/ (gu), /or/ (ar), /or/ (
Useful words: eye, hou

Aran the Home Visit Pharmacist

Aran helps people stay healthy. Join him on his visits!

Non-fiction
**Real-life hero:
Pharmacist**

Other books you might like:

Adil the Wind Farm Fixer
> **Aran the Home Visit Pharmacist**
Firefighter Frida

OXFORD
UNIVERSITY PRESS

www.oup.com

web   www.oxfordprimary.com
email primary.enquiries@oup.com
tel   +44 (0)1536 452610

ISBN 978-1-382-02952-

9 781382 029520

Mamba
and the crocodile bird

Written by Frances Usher

Illustrated by Stephen Lewis

Heinemann